THOUGHTS UNTHOUGHT

A BOOK FOR SELF-EXPLORATION

ADITYA SINGH

Special thanks to my parents for always motivating me to achieve whatever I want to

ഇ

Love you MAA

Thank you Precious*

Contents

Foreword

This book contains a compilation of completely random thoughts that have no relation to one another. The book is organized into 16 chapters, each with 12 thoughts; it is intended to assist you with lucid dreaming by presenting some extremely evocative thoughts to help you kickstart your passive dream state.

Each chapter is titled after some of history's most bizarre individuals, places, and events, which will aid you in evaluating the success of each chapter and your subconscious control.

Every chapter name appears to be completely random, but trust me when I say that it isn't. It has to do with the balance of your mental state. Before proceeding within the chapter, the story of behind the chapter's name should be learned first provided in the end. Because the information learned can be upsetting, reading the entire chapter will help you balance your thoughts and manipulate your subconscious ideas.

> *"Some of this stories can be very disturbing for a specific category of audience so I removed the part where a described about each title however you can search about them on the internet"*

I

Desmond Doss

I didn't exist in your world until you started reading this line

Antarctica is statistically the best place to have a baby because all 11 babies born there, lived making it have a zero percent infant mortality rate

There are only 365 different birthdays for nearly 8 billion people and we still find it difficult to find people with the same birthdate

Sleep is just a free trial of death and to be honest if you live to be around 80 you would have spent a third of your life sleeping

TV shows generally have fake laugh tracks in their background so you know when to laugh at a really bad joke

ꝏ

While you sleep you're just looking at the back of your eyelids for eight hours straight

ꝏ

While drinking water normally in a glass, we empty our drink from the top on the other hand using a straw empties it from the bottom

ꝏ

There have been entire civilizations who never knew that water had a solid form

ꝏ

The money you earned is never actually yours; it's just your turn with it and would one day be passed to someone else

ꝏ

A jail in a prison are basically the same thing but a jailer and a prisoner are completely different

ꝏ

When you say the word 'forward' your lips move forward; when you say the word 'back' your lips move back

ꝏ

If you try to rob a bank you shouldn't have any problems with rent or food bills for the next 10 years regardless of whether or not you're successful in robbing it

II

Hirohito

It is weird that blue is usually seen as cold while red is usually seen as hot but blue fire is hotter than red fire

Neuroscience is the study of the brain by the brain; it's the study of the brain learning about itself

Your hands are really just your brain's personal servants to interact with what it perceives to be real

If the universe is a simulation it might explain insomnia as a no space error in the sleeping server

The only way you can know you've fallen asleep is by waking up

Life is actually just generations of kids disciplining other kids hoping that the next group does just a little bit better

ꟽ

What if plants were just farming us, giving us the necessary oxygen we need to survive until about 100 years later when we ultimately die, our bodies get thrown back into the soil, where plants can then consume us

ꟽ

If anyone says you're useless just know you're helping keep everyone else alive just by existing and breathing

ꟽ

The evolution of all life is literally the story of planets developing oceans and then eventually watching those oceans get up and start walking around

ꟽ

When you're reading, you're literally looking at a dead tree and hallucinating

ꟽ

Every book you've ever read is just a remix of the dictionary

ꟽ

If you had one dollar for every year that the universe has existed (approximately 13.8 billion years) you wouldn't even make the top 50 on the Forbes list

III

Taufa'ahau Topou

If two mind readers are reading each other's minds whose mind are they actually reading?

You have seen Moon's surface more than Earth's land

We aren't afraid of being alone in the dark, we're afraid of the exact opposite

Our parents taught as not to talk with strangers but the only way to make friends is to literally talk to strangers

If a serial killer is chasing you, you're both literally running for your life

If you randomly drew some stars on a page your drawing is probably a very accurate representation of some particular cluster of stars in the sky

ꙮ

A major part of our population doesn't know that Picasso was alive when the titanic sank and at the same time he was also alive to witness the first moon landing on television

ꙮ

The light of the moon is just a reflection of the sun so how come vampires don't burn at night

ꙮ

Belts are probably some of the dirtiest items of clothing, people always touch them after they've used the bathroom but think about it, when was the last time you washed a belt

ꙮ

The amount of dirt and smudges that end up on spectacles is literally a visual representation of what could have ended up in our eye.

ꙮ

Sneezing seems to defy the laws of physics as our head is propelled forward when we sneeze instead of backwards

ꙮ

We see diamonds as precious and valuable but in universal terms, Wood is the most precious items to find

IV

Zhang Zongchang

When I was younger, I used to love waiting for the tooth fairy; it was the one chance I got to sell my body without child protective services knocking on my parent's door

Pigeons can actually distinguish human faces. But to be honest, I'm pretty sure most people couldn't even identify a pigeon

Why are humans scared of getting bitten by spiders when we have more teeth than them? And why are spiders scared of getting stomped on by humans when they have more legs?

For some reason, lemons, limes, lemon soda, lime soda, and lemon lime soda all taste completely different from one another

A fresh fruit salad is a modern technological wonder that is often overlooked. Think about it, at what point in human history could you ever have one spoon that contained fruits from multiple countries, climates, and even continents?

Don't feel bad about your handwriting, on the bright side, you have your own unique font

Our generation thinks they're doing much more than any other generation did to change things for the better, when in reality, only future generations can say whether that's the case or not

Earth's population has doubled in the past 50 years but it took almost 2 million years to get to the 3.7 billion human population in 1971

You've probably done some really weird stuff in somebody else's dream

11% is both 1% and 10% more than 10%

The 60s were now 60 years ago we're also as close to the 70s in the past as we are to the 70s in the future

It’s funny to notice that "I’ll be there in 17 minutes" sounds super specific but saying "I’ll be there in 15 minutes" sounds super generic

V

James Patrick Bulger

A lethal dose of something is also technically a lifetime supply

Sandwich is just an item of food consisting of two pieces of bread with some filling in between so by definition loaves of bread that we buy are really just massive bread sandwiches

You would probably say 0.6 as "zero point six" but in reality it's "zero point sixty"

Since a meteor killed off a dominant species on earth millions of years ago aren't we technically living in a post-apocalyptic world right now

Dogs are able to legally pee in more places than we are

ꙮ

If you look at yourself in a mirror from five feet away aren't you technically seeing yourself from ten feet away?

ꙮ

Light takes time to travel you're also technically looking at yourself slightly in the past

ꙮ

Saying I sold an hour of my life for $15 sounds a lot worse than I make $15 an hour

ꙮ

If cigarette companies cured cancer, cigarette sales will proudly increase which makes everyone happy in the end

ꙮ

Saying "Have a nice day" to someone sounds super friendly and is pretty normal but i don't know why but saying "Enjoy your next 24 hours" sounds threatening

ꙮ

Why is it so awkward walking back after you bowl?

ꙮ

Our senses are kind of crazy, our eyes can detect nuclear fusion happening trillions of miles away

VI

Ariadna Gutierrez

Captchas are hillariously just a robot asking us if we are of their kind

ℵ

The great thing about artificial intelligence is that it does exactly what you want it to do but the bad thing about artificial intelligence is that it does exactly what you want it

ℵ

Even if phones and other electronics became waterproof most of us will still probably subconsciously avoid getting anything wet

ℵ

If elevators haven't been invented all the CEOs and important people would probably have their offices on the first floor as a sign of status instead of the highest floor

ℵ

The most massive glass towers in the world are in a way the world's tallest sand castles

ꕥ

It's weird that if a small business is family-owned, people see it as friendly but if a large company is owned by family, it smells like corruption

ꕥ

Your brothers and sisters are just alternate versions of what could have been you

ꕥ

Has anyone ever seen a taxi at a gas station before because I swear I've never seen one

ꕥ

People say life is short but that phrase usually encourages people to do things that will probably make their life shorter

ꕥ

Percentages are reversible for example 80% of 30 is equal to 30% of 80

ꕥ

When we write with a pencil on a paper on a wooden desk we are actually using a dead tree to place a dead tree to be written on with another dead tree

ꕥ

Alarm clocks are one of the only devices that make you angry in both scenarios whether they work or not

VII

Alan Turing

How many sides does a piece of paper have? It's actually six you won't realize it until you start stacking

ꟹ

Your parents told you not to talk to strangers but it's the only way to make friends and progress in life

ꟹ

One nice thing about the internet is that you can pretty much get in an argument with an 8 year old and leave feeling superior

ꟹ

At some point, the internet will be older than all humans alive

ꟹ

Our future generations will have tons of high quality video footage of so many extinct animals, old civilizations who used to live before the arctic melted and disappeared

ꟸ

It must've been really awkward being the first historian to have ever existed

ꟸ

The number of people older than you never increases, it only decreases

ꟸ

Normally the floors are what stops gravity from killing us but if we get too far away from it gravity uses the floor to kill us

ꟸ

Trains were invented in 1804; Every human in that era who ever lived the experience to speed upwards of 56 miles per hour was falling to their deaths

ꟸ

Life is short so they say but life is only short if you love your life otherwise it is very very painfully long

ꟸ

Life is like playing a game where it is more painful to lose the game by 1, then by 100 points

ꟸ

Good dreams are basically a free trial of the life you could've been living

VIII

14th April 1561

When you scroll on your phone, nothing changes except for the color of the pixels on your screen giving an illusion of movement

ഇ

A little broken brushing your teeth is really the only time you ever clean your skeleton

ഇ

You really can't clean something without making anything else dirty; Cleaning is just rearranging dirt

ഇ

We can't move our top teeth and we cant say 'hum' while holding our nose shut also we can't snap our fingers inside our mouth

ഇ

As kids 99.9 percent of the times we cried was due to physical pain, as adults though 99.9% of the times people cry is due to emotional pain

ꕥ

In a hospital, you can find people experiencing the worst, the happiest, the first or the last days of their lives

ꕥ

Your right elbow is and will forever remain untouched by your right hand

ꕥ

Have you ever realized that the word 'short', 'shorter' and 'shortest' are actually just the long, longer and longest versions of the word 'short'

ꕥ

Nothing is ever on fire, it's fire that is on things but don't worry you can put the fire out by putting the right things on fire

ꕥ

When you're drinking any alcoholic drink both you and the drink get drunk

ꕥ

You spend your entire life collecting people for your funeral

ꕥ

You have no idea if you've lived 20% of your life or 90% of your life as you lifespan is not yet known

IX

Leopold Lojka

Some people think wisdom teeth are useless but it is actually the reason some oral surgeons are able to make a living

ᘓ

Some people work the same job for their entire life wondering what could have been like if they're taking a slightly different path

ᘓ

It's crazy that some people have more money than their brain cells

ᘓ

There's a certain point in everyone's life where how high can you count changes from a matter of knowledge to matter of will

ᘓ

The brain named itself and the funny part is now it is surprised to know it

Some stranger somewhere still remembers you because you were kind of them when no one else was

You can almost universally and instantaneously stress out any person just by shouting "Hey catch!"

There was a moment when your mom or dad picked you up as a baby and put you down only to never pick you up again

Most of us will receive their first bunch of flowers only at our funeral

There is only one letter to differentiate between creation and cremation which have exact opposite meanings

Passwords have probably stopped more people from getting into their own accounts then hackers; having the opposite effect that it was intended to have

People who were sentenced to house arrest in 2020 really lucked out timing wise

X

Jogendranath Mondal

Gambling is only considered an addiction if you're bad at it otherwise you're considered lucky

A lot of Google's revenue comes from people that are just too lazy to type .com after the end of their search

It doesn't matter how many fishes are there in the sea, if you don't know how to fish

The night before you have a day off is like 100 times better than the actual day off itself because you're already worried about the next day when you have to go back

There's a lonely piece of paper that's been in the same printer tray for years and years on end simply because the paper is always loaded on top of it

---

We're all losers in the race of time but I really want to see if I can make a slinky go down an escalator forever

---

It takes more letters to spell the word 'short' than it does to spell 'long'

Everyone tends to consider the question that where do we go after death but never asks where were we before birth

---

You've probably walked past someone that you played video games with online before and just didn't realize it

---

It's interesting that the two richest people on our planet are actively building businesses to build rockets to get off this planet

---

The richest person on earth is technically also the richest person in the universe since our definition of rich is owning a lot of earth money

---

The first parents to ever have identical twins must have been really really confuse

XI

Grigori Rasputin

If tailfins are the only things to differentiate between a human and a mermaid then lobsters are mermaids for scorpions

Attractive people think the world is a lot more polite than it actually is

The sinking of the Titanic must be a miracle for the fishes that were gonna be cooked the next morning

Our stomach thinks all potatoes are mashed

When you drink alcohol you are just borrowing happiness from tommorrow

Social media is the biggest graveyard of dead people it's ironic that there would one day be more people on social media than in real world

ഇ

Aren't we just a penis. The rest of our body is to make sure that our penis survives to make more penises

ഇ

If our shirt isn't tucked to our pants then our pants are tucked into our shirts

ഇ

Childbirth is literally an emergency in our world

ഇ

If a preganant woman starts swimming can we call her a human submarine

ഇ

We will never hear about a truly perfect crime

ഇ

The word "Fat" just looks like someone took a bite out of the word "Eat"

ഇ

The only time the word "incorrectly" isn't spelled incorrectly is when it's spelled incorrectly

XII

Ota Benga

When you look at the moonlight reflecting off from a water body, you're seeing light coming from plasma, reflected off by a solid that was then refracted by a gas and then ultimately reflected by a liquid to reach your eyes

ꙮ

Your tongue somehow knows exactly how everything you look at will feel

ꙮ

You really don't understand, how strong you chew until you accidentally bite your own tongue

ꙮ

The heart is basically a timer counting down until your death

ꙮ

There's a chance that the last picture of yourself you took could also end up being the one that is used for your obituary

ꝏ

How famous do you have to be to actually be assassinated as opposed to just being murdered

ꝏ

The baby's age is only counted after being born is a fetus that is still inside the womb technically a negative age

ꝏ

Humans are the only species that decided that water was too boring of a beverage to keep us alive

ꝏ

Have you ever thought about the fact that your belly button is technically your first mouth

ꝏ

The same conspiracy theorists that believe low-quality footage of the oppose are the same people who don't believe HD footage of rocket landings

ꝏ

What's the point in calling it reality TV if almost everyone in the world knows it's fake

ꝏ

A lot of times bad ideas aren't really bad ideas they're just least frequently talked about

XIII

January 23, 1556

Inventions are only created to increase or prevent laziness

I wonder if there's any times in a clock I haven't seen before

Is blinking the plural of winking

Being able to go to sleep without worrying that you'll get eaten by some random animal is probably the most privileged thing about our modern world

We only care about our body when we are sick

The fact that people can convince themselves that meeting aliens would go smoothly is nothing short of pure hoping

Hospital is simultaneously the building where most people leave without entering and also the building where most people enter without leaving

Kids don't really enjoy sleeping because they haven't gotten bored with life yet

The easiest way to tell if you're obese is by asking a kid to draw your stick figure

The 2 main colors of the traffic light red and green when those are the 2 colors the most color blind people can differentiate

Often times we're told that life is a game, well if that's true does that mean that pregnant women are game developers

You'll understand what pretty privileges are when you notice how you treat moths versus the way you treat butterflies

XIV

Tarrare

Barbie has more movies in the entire Marvel cinematic universe (Don't ask me how I know that)

Human milk is one of the few things that almost every single human being on the planet has tasted but also the one thing that no one remembers the taste of

Every joke has a hidden timer and if you don't laugh before the timer expires it's no longer funny

Man's greatest problems are caused by our intelligence which is also what solves most of our problems

The floppy disk disappeared from this world years ago but we still use it as a logo for most data storage stuff

The International Space Station basically takes the smartest people on earth and stops them from being the smartest people on earth

Everyone says practice makes perfect but in reality it's not because a doctor writes medicine their whole lives but still end up writing a prescription like the 3 year old kids who can hold a crayon this shows that doing something 1 million times in a row doesn't make you any better than a kid coloring outside of the lines for the thousandth time in a row. In reality it takes conscious effort into trying to improve to actually improve in something

You have the same amount of gold medals as the majority of people who go to the Olympics

Michael Collins was the loneliest mankind has ever been by going to the other side of the moon for 47 minutes without any human or radio connection

We've named the colors to give us a way to communicate and reference them, but in reality, there's no way of knowing that what you see is the same as what another person sees.

Countries that are bordered by water use something called "coastlines" to mark their territory. The coast is the land along the sea, and the boundary between the coast and the sea known as a coastline but the coastlines are changing due to global warming. So i don't know but it doesn't make sense to mark country boundaries with it

XV

Blanche Monnier

You wake up in the morning, head outside, and you say "good morning" to your next door neighbor. You walk down the street and you see a familiar face; you nod to let them know that you acknowledge them. You get into the bus and an old lady walks in behind you, so you stand and let her take your seat. You're not compelled to do any of these things. It's not in any constitution or any written rulebook. But somehow, we all follow these rules and we all know when someone breaks them

ꕤ

If you're close enough to people, you'll most likely know all of the details without asking. And if you're not close enough to them to know, then you're not close enough to be asking either

ꕤ

There is no need to point out someone's mistakes if it can't be fixed immediately. Doing so would only make the person insecure and self-conscious

ꕤ

There are two places you should never make a fuss or start drama, a wedding and at a funeral

ꕤ

Some rules of the society are just unspoken but you need to follow them. If everyone and everything was to be put in a constitution, won't we be living like robots

ꕤ

Every time you paint a room, it gets a little bit smaller

ꕤ

Every time you smell something, it gets a tiny bit lighter

ꕤ

When you go flying in an airplane, people say, "Have a safe flight" but you literally have no control if the plane flies safely or not

ꕤ

Open your contact list and you would get to know how much people actually love to talk to you

ꕤ

In horror movies, why is it always the piano that's the haunted, pretentious, scary instrument?

ꕤ

Shouldn't you take autograph of every person who works his ass of to be successful, you never know if he becomes the next Edison or the next Michael Jackson

ꕤ

We fear death by an airplane crash but after exiting the airport we catch a taxi, an act that is nearly a 100 times more likely to result in your death

Ishi

Was fire a "discovery" or an "invention"?

One day we weren't, today we are, and one day we will be no more

Why is yawning contagious?

Crying activates our parasympathetic nervous system and helps return our bodies to a normal fully functional state. It's a good thing for your body, so why do we associate it with such sad things?

There are some very popular opinions that all of us have collectively agreed to be true, even though they are in fact not and has been titled as "scientific facts"

Everything in space is falling... in every direction imaginable, all at the same time. The only reason it seems as if you're floating and not falling is because space is very large and mostly very empty

❧

We have heard stories of an apple falling on Newton's head leading to his discovery of gravity but in fact it is not true. We made that story to help us feel better about ourselves. When we believe that some of humanity's greatest achievements couldn't have happened without a huge slice of luck, we can keep hope alive for our own share of luck

❧

The brain is just 3% of the body's weight, but it uses 20% of the body's energy

❧

As a species, we continue to make assumptions about everything we see, and chances are, most of it'll be wrong. But that's a good thing, because if we never know what's wrong, we can never know what's truly right

❧

The very first commercial smartphone was released around 30 years ago, but it wasn't until 2007 with the release of the iPhone, that phones truly became smart by modern standards

❧

Before phones were invented, we always had to visit each other unannounced. But since phones came around and texting became a thing, we don't go to people's houses without texting or calling them to let them know

There are two people you should never lie to; your doctor and your lawyer

Software Algorithms are great. They bring everything we want right to our doorsteps, but I think they are slowly beginning to dictate our lives

Credits

"A lot of information provided in this book is inspired from the blog articles by Aperture and CodeCeTra"

About Aperture :-

Aperture is producing video essay style content on YouTube for an audience of over 1,400,000 subscribers. Video topics include science, technology, psychology, sociology, and everything else the Universe has to offer.

Website :- www.aperture.gg

ꟸ

About CodeCeTra :-

Whether you are an experienced web designer or a complete newbie, CodeCeTra will have something for you. We provide a range of free tutorials and other literature to help you with starting your exciting coding journey.

Website :- www.codecetra.in

9 798886 295986

Printed by Libri Plureos GmbH in Hamburg,
Germany